Beautiful Little Star

Written by Sylva Nnaekpe

Copyright © 2019 Sylva Nnaekpe.

All rights reserved. No part of this book may be reproduced by any means, medium, graphic, electronic or mechanical, including photocoping, recording, taping or by any information storage retrival system without the written permission of the author except in the case of brief quotations embodied in critical articles and reviews.

Books may be ordered through bookstores or
by contacting Silsnorra Publishing at:
silsnorra@gmail.com

Due to the dynamic nature of the internet, any web address or links contained in this book may have changed since publication and may no longer be valid. The views expressed in this work are solely those of the author and do not necessarily reflect the views of the publisher, and the publisher hereby disclaims any responsibility for them.

ISBN: 978-1-951792-05-3 (Soft Cover)
ISBN: 978-1-951792-06-0 (Hard Cover)
ISBN 978-1-951792-29-9 (Electronic book)

Printing information available on the last page.

Silsnorra Publishing Review Date: 10/18/2019

My birth ushered in happiness, joy, and laughter. It was the most beautiful sight to behold.

I have the most beautiful features: hair, eyes, nose, ears, teeth, and mouth—just like other people.

My heart is full of compassion, love, and care. I have a mind I can call my own.

I am a free spirit—willing, able, and ready to learn and explore new things.

Blood runs in my veins, and I go through the same process of growth and development as most other kids. I learn to crawl, talk, sit, stand, walk, and run, just like many of the children I meet.

I enjoy the gifts of life—air, water, food, drink, sunlight, the stars, the sands, and the seasons—just like everyone else.

I have lots of energy. I am clothed to suit the seasons, and I am a cool kid. I am surrounded by people who care and want to see me do well.

I will grow up to be whatever I want and choose to be, with the help and support of the people who love me, care about me, and are around me.

I am loved, and I care. Some things may try to tear us apart, but I am confident that together, we can make the world better than it is now.

My name is Ivry.

I am beautiful,

and

so are you.

THE END

Follow@ ivrydbook
to see more.

www.ingramcontent.com/pod-product-compliance
Lightning Source LLC
Chambersburg PA
CBHW051403110526
44592CB00023B/2938